The **SEO** *Wizard*

UNLOCK THE POWER OF ORGANIC SALES

A Book Written by *George Liontos*

A few words about me

My name is Liontos Georgios I have been working in the field of Programming and Online Marketing for more than 10 years.

In recent years I have established my own Digital Marketing Agency called Web-Net in which we undertake customers who have advertising needs and improve their Online presence.

Having studied computer science from an early age I discovered my love for Online Marketing and all the techniques around it.

I will try in some pages to convey to you as much as possible and better information about SEO or Search Engine Optimization and in Greek search engine optimization.

Why is this eBook worth reading?

You've probably heard a hundred times that Search Engine Optimization (SEO) is a vital digital marketing tool, but even if you have a basic understanding of what it entails, you may not yet have a strong understanding of this complex and multifaceted issue.

SEO is made up of many different elements and knowing what it is and how it works is the key to understanding why SEO is so important. In short, SEO is important because it makes your site more visible and that means more traffic and more opportunities to convert visitors into customers.

Beyond that, it is also a valuable tool for brand awareness, building relationships with prospects and positioning yourself as a credible and trusted expert in your field.

So, without further ado, here is everything you need to know about SEO and why it is so important in today's digital world. In this eBook you will find in detail all the steps that will help you win a place on the Google podium.

Welcome to the first complete SEO guide.

Table of Contents

CHAPTER ONE

Introduction

You will get the best from this guidebook if your drive to understand (SEO) search engine optimization is actually exceeded your willingness to perform and test concepts.

This book is created to summarize almost all main facets of SEO, from discovering the terms and phrases (keywords) which may bring qualified visitors to your site, and make your search friendly engines, to link building and advertising the special value of your website.

The world of search engine marketing is an ever-changing and complex, though you are able to quickly understand the fundamentals, and even a tiny quantity of SEO understanding, this can make a huge impact. Free SEO learning is also widely on the net, including in guides like this! (Woohoo!)

Incorporate this info with some exercise, and you're best on your way to being a savvy SEO.

The fundamentals of online search engine optimization

Ever heard of Maslow's hierarchy of needs? It is a principle of psychology that prioritizes the most essential human needs (like air, water, and physical safety) over higher needs (like self-esteem and social belonging). The principle is the fact that you cannot achieve the requirements at the summit without ensuring the more basic requirements are met first.

As you are able to observe, the basis of great SEO starts with making sure crawl accessibility and also moves up from there.

CHAPTER TWO

What's SEO, and why is it important?

In case you currently have a great knowledge of SEO and the reason it is important, For everybody else, this particular chapter can help develop your foundational SEO understanding and confidence as you move ahead.

What's SEO?

SEO stands for "search engine optimization." It is the process of boosting both quality and volume of site traffic and exposure to the brand name through non-paid (also known as an "organic") search engine results.

Note, despite the acronym, SEO is just as much about people as it's about search engines themselves. It is about realizing what people are looking for online, the answers they're seeking, the terms they use, and the content type they would like to ingest. Understanding the answers to these thoughts is going to allow you to hook up with the individuals who are searching online for all the solutions you offer.

If understanding your audience's intent is one aspect of the SEO coin, delivering it in how yahoo crawlers are able to locate and also understand will be the other person. In this ebook guide, you will figure out how to do both.

Search engines are answer machines. They scour enormous amounts of pieces of content and evaluate thousands of elements to decide what written content is almost certainly to answer your query.

Search engines do this by identifying and also cataloging all accessible information on the Internet (the web pages, PDFs, pictures, etc.) via a procedure referred to as indexing "and" crawling and after ordering it by just how nicely it complements the query in a procedure we talk about as "ranking." We will cover ranking, indexing, and crawling in much more information within the next chapter.

2.1 What search results could be "organic"?

As we stated previously, organic search results are ones that are attained through highly effective SEO, not paid out for (i.e., not advertising).

Nowadays, search engine results pages - known as "SERPs" - are loaded with both much more advertising and more powerful natural results formats (called "SERP features") than we have already seen before. Several good examples of SERP features are featured snippets (or respond boxes), People Also Ask boxes, image carousels, and so on. New SERP features consistently emerge, driven mostly by what people are looking for.

For instance, in case you look for "Denver weather," you will see a weather forecast for the city of Denver straight in the SERP rather than an URL to a website that could have that forecast. Plus, in case you look for "pizza Denver," you will see a "local pack" result comprised of Denver pizza places. Handy, right?

It is crucial to remember that search engines earn money from advertising. Their objective is to better solve searcher's queries (within SERPs), to also keep searchers coming back again, and then to have them on the SERPs for longer period.

Some SERP features on Google are natural and also may be affected by SEO. These include featured snippets (a promoted natural result that displays a solution inside a box) and similar questions (a.k.a. like "People Also Ask" boxes).

Note, it is well worth noting that there are lots of other search features that, although they are not really a paid advert, cannot generally be affected by SEO. These characteristics frequently have information acquired from proprietary information resources, like Wikipedia, WebMD, and IMDb.

2.2 Why SEO is crucial

While paid advertising, social media, along with any other internet platforms, are able to generate traffic to sites; note the vast majority of internet traffic is pushed by an online search engine.

Organic search results deal with more digital real estate, appear much more credible to savvy searchers, and also get way more clicks than paid advertisements. For instance, of all US searches, just 2.8 % of people click are paid advertisements.

In a nutshell: SEO has ~20X more traffic opportunities than PPC on both mobile and pc.

SEO is also among the only online advertising channels that, when put together properly, can continue paying dividends in the long run. In case you present a great bit of content that deserves to get ranking for the proper keywords, your website traffic is able to snowball over time, whereas marketing needs constant funding to drive visitors to your website.

The search engines are getting smarter, though they still want our help.

Optimizing your website can help supply much better info to search engines; therefore, your content could be correctly indexed and also shown within search results, should I use an SEO expert, consultant, or company?

According to your bandwidth, willingness to discover, so the intricacy of your respective website(s), you can conduct some simple SEO yourself. Or, you may discover that you'd like the assistance of an expert. One or the other way is acceptable!

Should you wind up searching for expert assistance, it is crucial that you understand that many companies and consultants "provide SEO services" but can differ widely in quality. Understanding how to choose a very good SEO company can help you save a lot of money and time, as the bad SEO techniques can, in fact, harm your site a lot more than they'll help.

CHAPTER THREE

Basic SEO, checklist

The best way to utilize this particular SEO checklist, most SEO checklists doesn't talk just about how SEO is a continuing process. Rather, they list random activities and also make it seem as SEO is performed and dusted the moment you check them off.

That is not the case; therefore, we have provided each product on our checklist among these tags:

- Do it once
- Do it periodically
- Do it every time you post a brand-new page.

This structure means you do not have to search through everything on this checklist today. Do the one-time jobs first, then the regular jobs, now finish the ongoing things every time you post a new webpage.

Let us get into it.

SEO basics checklist let us start with a number of SEO best practices everybody ought to have in the bag. These will not directly improve positions, though they are crucial in setting yourself up to get ranked much higher in Google.

1. Set up Google Search Console

Google Search Console is a totally free application for monitoring your website's organic search performance.

Allow me to share a couple of things you are able to do with it:

- See the key phrases you rank for
- Check ranking positions
- Find site errors
- Submit sitemaps

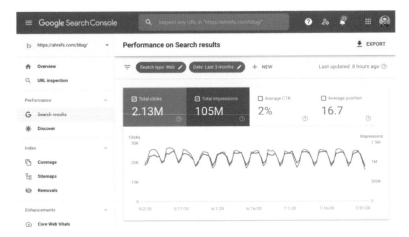

2. Put together Bing Webmaster Tools

Bing Webmaster Tools is basically Bing's equivalent of Google Search Console.

3. Put together Ahrefs Webmaster Tools

Ahrefs Webmaster Tools (AWT) is a totally free application that will help you boost your website's SEO performance for much more natural search traffic.

Here are some key features:

- Scan your website for 100 SEO issues
- See all of your backlinks
- See all of the available key phrases you rank for

4. Set up Google Analytics

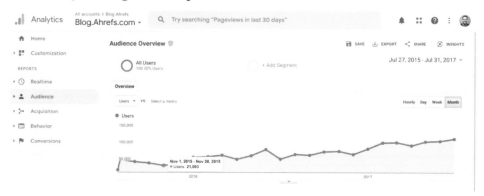

Google Analytics is a no-cost application that allows you to see the number of people who is visiting the website, where they are coming from, and the way they are interacting with it.

SIDENOTE

It is also well worth linking Google Search Console with Google Analytics to determine Search Console data in Analytics.

5. Install an SEO plugin

When you are utilizing WordPress, you will need an SEO plugin to enable you to optimize skin conditions as sitemaps and also meta tags.

Here are some good choices (you just need one):

- Yoast SEO
- Rank Math
- The SEO Framework

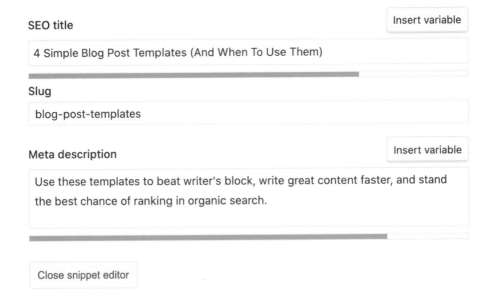

When you are using a different site platform like Shopify, you probably do not require an SEO plug-in.

6. Create and publish a sitemap

Sitemaps tell search engines where you can look for information that is crucial on your website so they can readily crawl and list your pages.

Here is what the sitemap is like for blog:

XML Sitemap

Generated by YoastSEO, this is an XML Sitemap, meant for consumption by search engines.

You can find more information about XML sitemaps on **sitemaps.org**.

This XML Sitemap contains 266 URLs.

URL	Images	Last Mod.
https://ahrefs.com/blog/archive/	0	2020-07-31 11:07 +00:00
https://ahrefs.com/blog/black-hat-link-building/	17	2016-03-01 10:44 +00:00
https://ahrefs.com/blog/going-viral/	35	2016-10-27 23:03 +00:00
https://ahrefs.com/blog/incredible-content/	23	2016-10-27 23:07 +00:00
https://ahrefs.com/blog/freelance-seo-career/	6	2016-10-27 23:19 +00:00
https://ahrefs.com/blog/seo-freelancing-lessons-learned/	6	2016-10-27 23:21 +00:00
https://ahrefs.com/blog/google-webmaster-forum-questions/	1	2016-10-27 23:23 +00:00
https://ahrefs.com/blog/public-data-sets/	20	2016-11-26 14:52 +00:00
https://ahrefs.com/blog/asking-for-tweets/	18	2017-01-25 08:50 +00:00
https://ahrefs.com/blog/the-ultimate-guide-to-reverse-engineering-your-competitors-backlinks/	18	2017-03-27 06:45 +00:00
https://ahrefs.com/blog/not-million-visit-organic-seo-case-study/	12	2017-03-29 13:51 +00:00
https://ahrefs.com/blog/whats-new-ahrefs-may/	10	2017-05-31 08:18 +00:00

You can typically find your sitemap at one of those URLs: /sitemap.xml

/sitemap_index.xml

/sitemap

7. Create a robots.txt file

Robots.txt is actually the basic text file that tells search engines exactly where they can and cannot go on your site.

It is good practice to get a robots.txt file, though It is a necessity in case you have to avoid search engines from crawling areas or pages on your website. For instance, in case you run an e-commerce store, you may not want them to examine and list your cart page.

You are able to check whether you currently have a robots.txt file by visiting yourdomain.com/robots.txt. If you notice a basic text file, you are all set. If you notice something else, search Google for "robots.txt generator" and make one.

CHAPTER FOUR

Technical SEO,
checklist

Technical SEO issues frequently keep a site back from ranking as high as it deserves. Listed here are the fundamental technical best practices everyone must follow.

1. Plan your site structure (new sites only)

It is essential that visitors and online search engines can easily navigate your site. That is the reason you have to make a logical site structure.

Use a Mind Map to Create Your Site Structure

To do this, drawing out a main map:

Each and every branch on the map must be an internal link to enable search engines and site visitors to go through between pages.

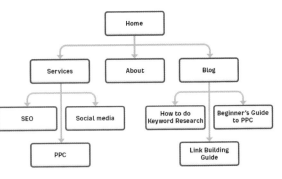

2. Make certain your website is crawl able

Google cannot read adequately index articles that are not crawl able; therefore, it is really worth checking out the Coverage report in Google Search Console for just about any alerts or exclusions associated with robots.txt.

If you would like Google to help, make sure Google indexes the blocked pages properly, you need to take away the principle that is creating the block out of your robots.txt file.

3. Ensure your website is index able

Indexing and crawling are two issues that are various. Just because search engines are able to crawl a page does not mean they can list it. When there is a' noindex' robots meta tag or x robots tag over the page, indexing is not feasible.

Details

Status	Type	Validation ↓	Trend	↓ Pages
Excluded	Excluded by 'noindex' tag	N/A	————	582

Google lets you know about noindexed URLs in the Coverage report.

You are able to also find the info within the Indexability report in Ahrefs' Site Audit.

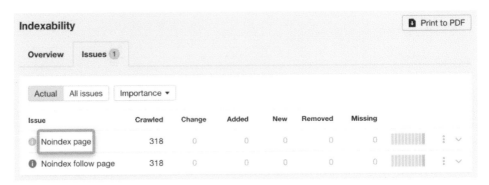

When you have' noindexed' pages that must be listed, take away the' noindex' tag.

4. Ensure you are using HTTPS

HTTPS is a confirmed little ranking factor.

Yeah, that is wrong. HTTPS isn't a factor in deciding if you should index a web page at all. We do use HTTPS as a lightweight ranking factor, and also, getting HTTPS is excellent for users. A free certification from Let us Encrypt works as well.

- 🐾 John 🐾 (JohnMu) January 29, 2019, If you are not utilizing HTTPS nowadays, it is time to help make the switch.

Potential ranking boosts aside, HTTPS is going to protect your visitors' information. This is particularly crucial in case you've any contact styles on your site. When you are requesting passwords or payment info, then it is not merely important; it is an absolute must.

How can you know whether your website uses HTTPS?

Search for a padlock inside your browser's search bar:

SIDENOTE.

You are able to buy a complimentary SSL certification from Let's Encrypt.

5. Ensure your site is accessible at one domain

Visitor should not be able to get access into your site at multiple places. It can lead to crawling, security issues, and indexing.

Request URL	Status codes
> http://ahrefs.com	301 200
> http://www.ahrefs.com	301 200
> https://www.ahrefs.com	301 200
> https://ahrefs.com	200

To check out that everything's as a way, plug these four URLs into httpstatus.io:

- http://www.yourdomain.com
- http://yourdomain.com
- https://yourdomain.com
- https://www.yourdomain.com

If that does not happen, you have to have a lasting 301 redirect.

If you are using HTTPS (you must be), it is also critical the accessible version of your site is the protected version. That is whether https://www.yourdomain.com or https://yourdomain.com.

6. Make certain your website loads fast

Page speed is a ranking factor on the desktop after 2010 as well as mobile after 2018.

It is not difficult to see why. It is annoying to click a search result and also have to hold out for doing it to load. That is why the likelihood of a bounce will increase as site speed decreases.

You are able to make use of resources as Gtmetrix and page speed Insights to find out just how quickly your web page loads.

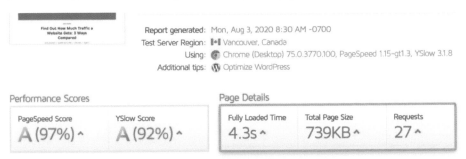

Nevertheless, these tools are only able to investigate one page at the same time.

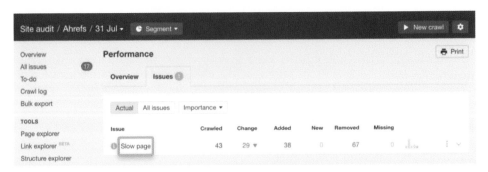

7. Make certain your website is mobile-friendly

Note most searches happen on mobile devices, so having a mobile-friendly website is more critical than ever.

Check whether your website needs to have work with Google's Mobile-Friendly Test tool.

8. Set up a picture compression plugin

Compressing images makes image files more compact and also increases page speed. That is crucial because site speed is a Google ranking factor.

When you are utilizing WordPress, there are loads of plugins for this. We love ShortPixel. It allows you to compress as many as 100 videos per month for totally free.

When you are making use of another site platform, search Google for a good plugin or use ShortPixel's web app.

9. Fix broken pages

Broken links could adversely influence user experience and break the flow of' authority' into and also around your site.

1. Crawl your site with Site Audit
2. Go to the Internal pages report
3. Look for "404 page" errors

Here is how you can cope with any broken links you find:

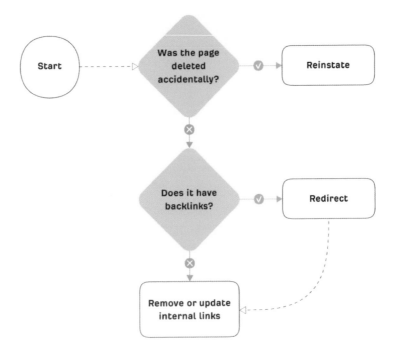

How to Deal
With Broken Links

10. Fix content duplicate issue

Duplicate exact content that appears up on the web in over one place. It is a typical e-commerce SEO issue because of faceted navigation. That by itself can cause hundreds of identical content issues.

You are able to find replicated content problems for free with Ahrefs Webmaster Tools.

1. Crawl your site with Site Audit
2. Go to the Duplicate content report
3. Hit the "Issues" tab

You can fix these by canonicalizing the affected URLs where it is necessary.

CHAPTER FIVE

Keyword Research
checklist

Keyword analysis is regarded as the essential piece of the SEO puzzle. When you do not understand what keywords, people are looking for, just how can you actually enhance your articles for an online search engine?

Follow these checklist things to get off in the right direction.

1. Find a key keyword to target

Every webpage on your site must focus on one main primary keyword. You must do keyword research periodically to discover keywords to focus on, though you must also ensure you are focusing on the very best keyword every time you post a brand-new webpage.

How can you tell which is the very best keyword?

It is the one that presents the most widely used method of searching for the subject.

For instance, let us say you are writing a post about the very best protein powders. There are plenty of ways people might look for this, such as:

- What is the very best protein powder?
- Best protein supplements
- Best protein shakes So that one of those key phrases do you focus on if any?

Fortunately, there is a great way to find this out. Simply look for your subject in Ahrefs' Keywords Explorer and check out the Parent Topic. This is normally a popular way of searching for the very same thing.

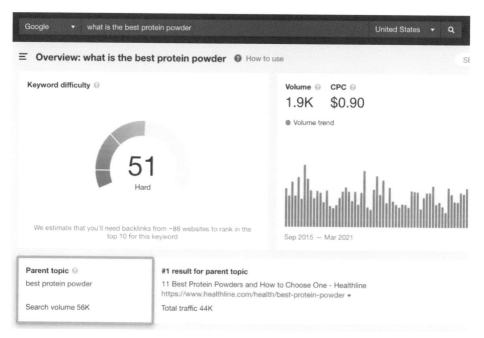

SIDENOTE

Parent Topic is not 100 % foolproof. It just shows the keyword sending most visitors to the top-ranking web page on your keyword. This is normally the very best keyword to target, although not always.

2. Assess search intent

Search intent is the reason for a searcher's query. If your post does not align with this, your likelihood of ranking is slim to none.

Just how do you evaluate search intent?

Look at the kinds plus structure of pages ranking in Google for your main keyword.

For instance, we are able to see from the URLs and titles of the top-ranking results for "marketing skills" that they are all blog posts. As for the format, they are mainly listicles.

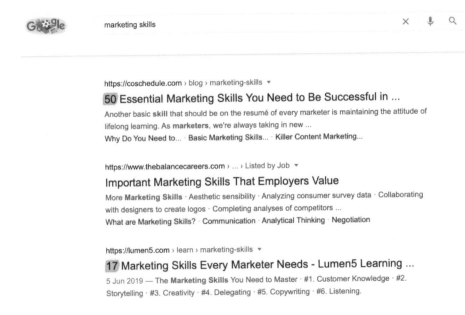

In case you targeted the keyword with a web page promoting a training course, you likely would not position it since it does not match search intent.

3. Assess your odds of ranking in Google

Realizing the ease or trouble of ranking for a search term allows you to prioritize the chance and set expectations that are realistic.

For a preliminary rough estimate, do the Keyword Difficulty score in Keywords Explorer.

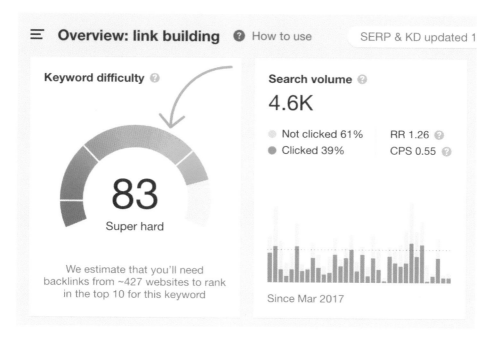

Keyword difficulty ❷

83

Super hard

We estimate that you'll need
backlinks from ~427 websites to rank
in the top 10 for this keyword

Search volume ❷

4.6K

Not clicked 61%   RR 1.26 ❷
Clicked 39%   CPS 0.55 ❷

Since Mar 2017

Simply do not depend on this entirely. Look at the success yourself for things which might suggest a tough key phrase to crack, like:

- High-quality backlinks to the top-ranking pages
- Predominantly huge makes in the top 10
- High topical importance of the top-ranking sites.

4. Research what people want to know

Let's say that somebody searches for "SEO keywords." You are able to see from analyzing search intention that individuals are searching for a meaning of the expression, but what some other issues do they've? And what much other info should you put in your information?

Google's "People Also Ask" box provides a little insight into this:

Your **SEO keywords** are the **keywords** and phrases in your web content that make it possible for people to find your site via search engines. A website that is well optimized for search engines "speaks the same language" as its potential visitor base with **keywords** for **SEO** that help connect searchers to your site.

www.wordstream.com › seo-keyword ▾

SEO Keywords: How to Find Keywords for Your Website ...

@ About Featured Snippets   📰 Feedback

People also ask

How do I find SEO keywords?   ⌄

How do I optimize keywords for SEO?   ⌄

Are keywords important for SEO?   ⌄

Feedback

For additional suggestions, take three top-ranking web pages and paste them into Ahrefs' Content Gap tool. This can demonstrate the key phrases that more than one of the papers ranks for.

Content Gap @ How to use

| ≣ 3 targets | Intersect: 3 ▼ | Volume ▼ | KD ▼ | CPC ▼ | Word count ▼ | Include keyw |

Show keywords that the below targets rank for

https://www.wordstream.com/seo-keyword	Prefix ▼
https://backlinko.com/hub/seo/seo-keywords	Prefix ▼
https://moz.com/learn/seo/what-are-keywords	Prefix ▼

+ Add target

⬤▬ At least one of the targets should rank in top 10

But the following target doesn't rank for

| | *.domain/* ▼ |

Show keywords

It is then only a situation of eyeballing the outcomes for search phrases that may represent subtopics, In our situation, which could be "keyword "how and examples" to use keywords for SEO."

Keyword	Volume ↓	KD	CPC	SERP	Highest position		
					https://www.	https://moz.c	https://backli
keywords	19,000	93	—	SERP ▾	4 ▾	3 ▾	10 ▾
seo keywords	5,100	91	7.00	SERP ▾	1 ▾	3 ▾	5 ▾
key words	3,100	93	1.70	SERP ▾	3 ▾	10 ▾	13 ▾
what are keywords	900	65	—	SERP ▾	6 ▾	1 ▾	12 ▾
seo keyword	600	95	10.00	SERP ▾	1 ▾	3 ▾	5 ▾
keywords for seo	400	90	6.00	SERP ▾	1 ▾	3 ▾	5 ▾
seo words	250	94	10.00	SERP ▾	4 ▾	3 ▾	14 ▾
website keywords	250	94	5.00	SERP ▾	1 ▾	5 ▾	20 ▾
keyword search engine	250	95	5.00	SERP ▾	4 ▾	6 ▾	12 ▾
web site keyword	200	96	7.00	SERP ▾	1 ▾	6 ▾	27 ▾
websites keywords	200	94	7.00	SERP ▾	1 ▾	8 ▾	19 ▾
keyword examples	200	61	—	SERP ▾	3 ▾	14 ▾	11 ▾
web site key words	200	94	7.00	SERP ▾	1 ▾	5 ▾	19 ▾
web site keywords	150	94	7.00	SERP ▾	1 ▾	5 ▾	19 ▾
keywords seo	150	91	8.00	SERP ▾	1 ▾	2 ▾	5 ▾
keyword seo	150	95	—	SERP ▾	1 ▾	2 ▾	5 ▾
examples of keywords	100	56	0.80	SERP ▾	6 ▾	12 ▾	11 ▾
search engine keywords	100	86	8.00	SERP ▾	2 ▾	1 ▾	5 ▾
how to use keywords for seo	100	78	6.00	SERP ▾	5 ▾	4 ▾	12 ▾
what keywords should i use	100	79	1.20	SERP ▾	3 ▾	6 ▾	12 ▾

CHAPTER SIX

Content checklist

Picking the proper key phrase is crucial, but your efforts are going to be in vain when your material is not up to scratch. Follow these points to level up your written content.

1. Solve the reader's problem

Understanding search intent may be the initial stage of fixing the reader's issue since it informs you of what content type they are searching for.

The study is another vital step.

But to make really good content, you have to go further and truly think about the visitor's problem.

For instance, have a query as "productivity tips." It is obvious from assessing search intent that searchers want a listicle-style blog post. And in case we investigate the top-ranking posts, we view typical advice as "take breaks" and "put things down on paper."

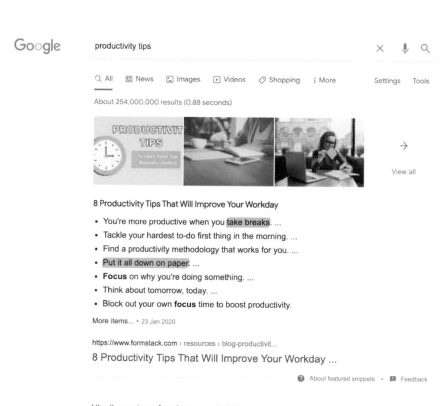

Although there is absolutely nothing that you do not like about these suggestions, people looking for "productivity tips" most likely need much more practical suggestions they're able to apply instantly.

So, you would most likely need to go beyond advice that is simple, like "take breaks."

2. Write a winning intro

In case you cannot convince readers that your post provides what they want within a number of seconds, they will hit that back button faster than you are able to say "dwell time."

Your greatest defense against this is a compelling intro.

Good introductions really should do three things:

1. Connect with the reader
2. Build trust
3. Promise an answer to the user's problem

Don't forget, if guests never get past your introduction, they never read your articles. And in case they don't read your articles, they will not turn, share, or link to them.

3. Use headings to generate a hierarchy

Headings as H2 and H1 help to produce hierarchy and bust your content into reasonable sections. This can make your material simpler to skim and digest.

For instance, the list that you are reading at this time is broken into five distinct sections.

- SEO basics checklist
- Technical SEO checklist
- Content checklist
- On-page SEO checklist
- Link building checklist

Under every one of these, we've sub subheadings for every checklist item.

Consider how much harder it will be reading this page with no subheadings.

4. Break things up with images

No person really wants to read a huge wall of text. It is overwhelming and can lead individuals to bounce.

Images can help to resolve this by breaking up your copy and aiding visual comprehension.

But do not only throw pictures in for the benefit of it. Make an attempt to find or create pictures that help the reader's knowledge.

For instance, we usually use screenshots, charts, and graphs to help you illustrate our points.

5. Use brief paragraphs and sentences

50 % of the US public hear below an 8th-grade reading level.

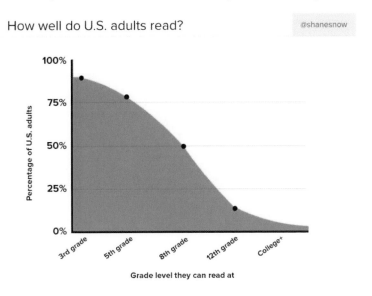

So unless you wish to alienate one half of the population, do not overcomplicate things. Stick to brief paragraphs and sentences.

You need to also:

- Avoid jargon
- Use easy words and phrases
- Write in a very active voice

Hemingway is a free, browser-based application that may assist you in particular. It informs you of the current quality level of your text and also suggests improvements.

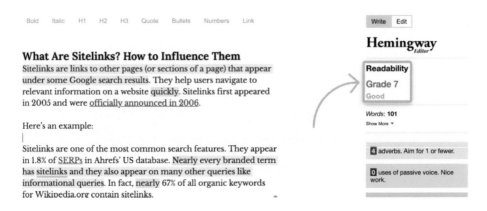

6. Include a table of contents

A table of contents offers jump links to various areas on the web page.

Even though you are able to include a table of contents to the web page, they are best suited to lengthy content that could normally be hard to navigate.

A table of contents may, in addition, enable you to succeed in site links in the SERPs.

https://ahrefs.com › blog › canonical-tags

Canonical Tags: A Simple Guide for Beginners - Ahrefs

What is a **canonical tag**? A **canonical tag** (rel="canonical") is a snippet of HTML code that defines the main version ...

14 Apr 2020 · Uploaded by Google Search Central

What a canonical tag looks... · Why canonical tags are... · Canonicalization best...

CHAPTER SEVEN

On Page SEO
checklist

On-page SEO is the procedure of optimizing the real information on your site. It provides optimizations made to visible content and content within

the source codes.

Let's consider how you can do it.

1. Use a short descriptive URL

Brief, descriptive URLs help searchers to realize what the webpage is about in the SERPs.

For instance, these two pages are about losing weight...

https://www.medicalnewstoday.com/articles/322345

https://www.dietdoctor.com/how-to-lose-weight

... but you would not know it from the first URL.

For the majority of the precious time, the easiest method to produce short, descriptive URLs is usually to set your main keyword as the URL slug.

ahrefs.com/blog/on-page-seo/

ahrefs.com/blog/link-building/

ahrefs.com/blog/free-seo-tools/

Keeping URLs short is beneficial because lengthy URLs have a tendency to truncate in the SERPs.

https://www.bloggingbasics101.com › how-do-i-start-a-...

How To Start a Blog in 2021 - Easy to Follow Guide for ...

5 Jan 2021 — Step 1 – Choose your preferred blogging platform · Step 2 – Self-hosting or a free alternative? · Step 3 – **Start a blog** on your own domain (if you ...

Blog Design: Keep It Clutter... · Advice for Blog Design and... · Blogging Resources

2 You need to write a compelling tag line

Like URLs, name-tags appear in Google's search engine results and also assist searchers in realizing what the webpage is about.

Common tips for title tags include your target keyword.

Although that is great thing to practise, do not sweat it if it does not make sense. It is a lot more crucial to create something strong that is going to make people want to press.

Most time your post or web page title works effectively.

3. Create a compelling meta description

Google shows meta explanations in the SERPs roughly ⅓ of the period.

Below are our best strategies for developing a compelling meta description:

- Expand on the title

- Double down on search intent
- Use an energetic voice
- Keep it under 120 characters
- Include your main keyword (where it will make sense)

4. Link to related resources

Connecting to other internal resources will help site visitors to navigate your site, but what about outside resources?

Here is what Google's John Mueller says:

Linking to various other sites is a good way to offer value for your users. Oftentimes, links help owners to discover more, to take a look at your sources, and also to better understand the way your material is applicable to the concerns that they've.

John Mueller, Search Advocate Google

Does it mean you've to force external and internal links into your articles?

Nope. Just add your links when it makes sense

5. Enhance your images

When you are using the checklist in order, you need to have installed a picture compression plugin. But there are a few different image optimizations you must do on a site by page basis:

1. Name images descriptively. Do not use generic image filenames as Screenshot-2021-06-01 or IMG_875939.png. Use descriptive filenames like eiffel-tower.jpg or black-puppy.png.
2. Add descriptive alt text. Alt text replaces a picture on the web page when it fails to load. It is also useful for those utilizing screen readers.

6. Add schema markup for rich snippets

Schema markup helps online search engines to understand your articles better. Though it is able to also dramatically impact the way, your post turns up in the SERPs.

Here is a site with schema markup which currently ranks for "pizza dough recipe:"

www.bbc.co.uk › food › recipes › pizzadoughbase_70980 ▾

Pizza dough recipe - BBC Food

 ★★★★★ Rating: 4.5 - 145 votes - 2 hrs 30 mins
Ingredients. 650g/1lb 7oz '00' flour (or strong white flour), plus extra for dusting. 7g dried easy-blend yeast. 2 tsp salt. 25ml/1fl oz olive oil. 50ml/2fl oz warm milk. 325ml/11fl oz warm water. passata and other toppings, for baking.

Here is what it will look like without schema markup:

www.bbc.co.uk › food › recipes › pizzadoughbase_70980 ▾

Pizza dough recipe - BBC Food

Ingredients. 650g/1lb 7oz '00' flour (or strong white flour), plus extra for dusting. 7g dried easy-blend yeast. 2 tsp salt. 25ml/1fl oz olive oil. 50ml/2fl oz warm milk. 325ml/11fl oz warm water. passata and other toppings, for baking.

Do you notice the difference?

Schema markup is able to increase click-through rates and bring more visitors to your site.

It is not that complex to implement either. Use Google's this Schema or markup helper markup generator to get it done with ease.

7. Add internal links

Internal links help Google find out what your post is about. Additionally, they help search engines and drivers to navigate your site.

We previously covered the benefits of linking applicable internal and external resources into your content. But it is also well worth adding internal links from various other related pages any time you publish brand new content.

Here is how you can look for related internal link opportunities:

1. Create a complimentary Ahrefs Webmaster Tools account
2. Crawl your site with Site Audit
3. Go on the Link Opportunities report
4. Add a "Target page" filter and configure it to your brand-new page

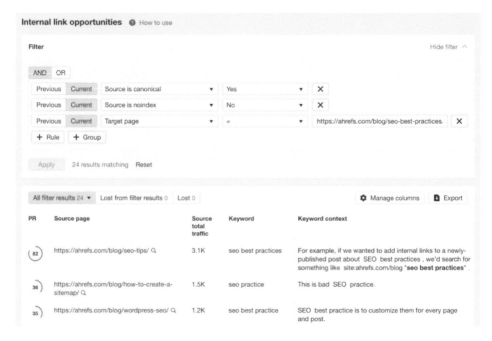

Add internal links to those pages anywhere it makes more sense.

CHAPTER EIGHT

Link Building checklist

Link building is an important SEO task, particularly in case you wish to get ranking for anything remotely competitive. In this particular area, we will discuss a number of tried and tested link-building practices.

SIDE NOTE.

Several of these strategies are centered on building inbound links to your site as a whole, whereas others can focus on building backlinks to specific pages.

1. Replicate your competitors' links

If a web page is bringing up and connecting to many competitors, but not you, it may be a website link really worth pursuing.

Here is how you can locate these sites:

1. Go to Content Explorer
2. Search for ("competitor 1" AND "competitor 2") "your brand"
3. Hit search
4. Toggle "One page per domain."

This can search our database of more than seven billion web pages for all those mentioning both your rivals, but not you.

Well, then it is simply a case of searching for opportunities in which you may might have the ability to get a link.

For instance, in case you are doing this for Convert Kit, this listing of 79 marketing equipment would possibly be a great opportunity:

79 Marketing Tools and Software for Every Business & Budget
https://blog.hubspot.com/marketing/marketing-tools ▾
The right marketing tool can make your job easier and increase performance as a result. We've got a roundup of... **MailChimp** 55. **AWeber** 56. ActiveCampaign Marketing Automation Tools Automation is nothing new to marketers.

Bethany Cartwright · 1 May 2017 · 2,601 words · 🐦 355 📌 403

2. Reclaim those lost links

Backlinks do not last forever.

For instance, in case we determine the Lost Links report in Ahrefs' Site Explorer for any Ahrefs Blog, we see plenty of lost backlinks within the last 7 days.

This occurs for all types of factors. Typically, they are gone for good. Other times it is achievable to reclaim them.

3. Pursue unlinked mentions

People will occasionally mention your brand without connecting to you. There're recognized as unlinked mentions.

Here is an instance of one:

You are able to find that although they mention Ahrefs, they do not link to us.

Today, would it not be awesome in case you could change unlinked mentions for the brand name to linked mentions?

It'd, and you are able to. Simply reach out to the writers and demand that they "make the text clickable." Because they are by now knowledgeable about your brand name, there is a great possibility that they will gladly make that change for you.

Nevertheless, the question remains: How can you discover unlinked brand mentions within the very first place?

All is defined in the guide below.

4. Publish guest posts

Guest blogging is exactly where you create and post an article on another website in your business.

For instance, here is a guest posting by Ryan Stewart on the Ahrefs Blog:

Hello. My name is Ryan Stewart and I'm a recovering black hat SEO.

I'm not ashamed to admit it. I used black hat methods because they worked. Really, really well.

I always wanted to go white hat, I just didn't have the manpower to scale. With 40+ clients demanding results, I did what what was needed to keep them happy.

Everything changed in 2014 when Google dropped the hammer on private blog

Ryan Stewart

My name is Ryan Stewart and I'm a digital marketing consultant with over 8 years of experience working with clients like Target, Accenture

The majority of people allow guest experts link to their site from their author bio.

You can find numerous ways to look for guest blogging opportunities, though a simple method is searching for sites that have previously written about related topics. Why? because those websites will probably be enthusiastic about a guest posting about a similar matter.

Here is how you can locate these sites:

1. Enter the relevant topic (e.g., "keyword research")
2. Go to Ahrefs' Content Explorer
3. Hit "Search"
4. Choose "In title" from the drop-down
5. Go on the "Websites" tab

Below you will visit the top 100 sites with probably the most natural traffic from web pages about your subject.

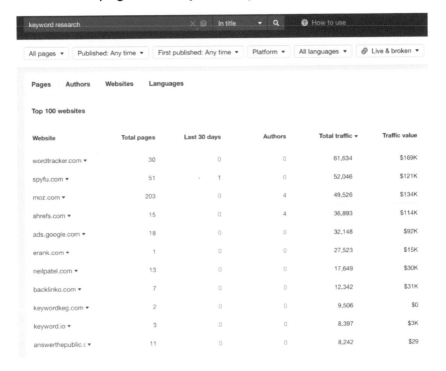

Website	Total pages	Last 30 days	Authors	Total traffic ▾	Traffic value
wordtracker.com ▾	30	0	0	61,634	$169K
spyfu.com ▾	51	1	0	52,046	$121K
moz.com ▾	203	0	4	49,526	$134K
ahrefs.com ▾	15	0	4	36,893	$114K
ads.google.com ▾	18	0	0	32,148	$92K
erank.com ▾	1	0	0	27,523	$15K
neilpatel.com ▾	13	0	0	17,649	$30K
backlinko.com ▾	7	0	0	12,342	$31K
keywordkeg.com ▾	2	0	0	9,506	$0
keyword.io ▾	3	0	0	8,397	$3K
answerthepublic.c ▾	11	0	0	8,242	$29

Search through the list and reach out to the pertinent sites.

5. Pitch resource pages

Resource pages are web pages that link and also curate information about a subject.

You are able to discover related resource pages using Google search operators like

- [topic] intitle: resources inurl: resources.html
- [topic] intitle:links URL: resources.html
- [topic] inurl:.com/resources
- [topic] inurl:resources intitle:resources

For instance, here is a source page listing digital marketing resource:

It will make sense to pitch an SEO aid for that list.

6. Find people connecting to inferior content

Assuming you have put some effort into producing the perfect piece of content in regards to a subject, there should be many posts that are not as good as yours.

People connecting to these posts are the best link prospects.

For instance, here is an article about long-tail keywords with an incorrect definition (it has absolutely nothing to actually do with length):

Long-Tail Keywords: A Better Way to Connect with Customers

Long-tail keywords are longer and more specific keyword phrases that visitors are more likely to use when they're closer to a point-of-purchase or when they're using voice search. They're a little bit counter-intuitive, at first, but they can be hugely valuable if you know how to use them.

If we can plug the post's URL into Site Explorer, we see its links from more than 1,000 sites.

Long-Tail Keywords: What They Are & How to Use Them | WordStream
www.wordstream.com/long-tail-keywords ▾

Ahrefs Rank [i]	UR [i]	DR [i]	Backlinks [i]	Referring domains [i]	Organic keywords [i]
1,469	56	90	3.76K +13 Recent 4.63K Historical 24.6K	1.09K Recent 1.18K Historical 2.27K	815 −28 PPC 0

So, we can very easily meet all those people, clarify the problem, and also recommend they link to our post about the long-tail keywords with a precise characterization instead.

How can you identify similar posts with plenty of backlinks?

Follow these steps:

1. Go to Content Explorer
2. Search for your topic (e.g., long-tail keywords)

3. Choose "In the title" from the fall down
4. Filter for web pages with a lot of referring domains (linking websites)

Well, then it is simply a case of locating a compelling reason someone must link to your site over theirs

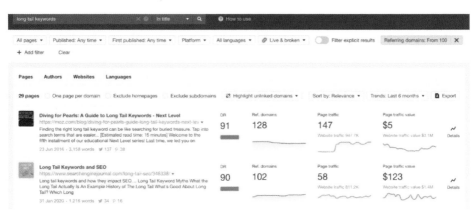

7. Let more people know about your content

People cannot link to the content in case they do not know it exists. That is exactly why you need to make a conscious attempt to tell the best? people about your articles.

But who are really the "right" people?

They've two attributes:

1. They are keen on your content
2. They have the capability to link to you

CHAPTER NINE

What's off page SEO

Off-page SEO describes each activity that takes place far from your site, which decides exactly where you position in the online search engine results pages (SERPs). Optimizing for off-site SEO ranking factors is essential for raising the relevance, authority, and trustworthiness of your site. This is mirrored in Google's algorithm components, with off-page SEO causing more than 50% of the ranking factors. Having a strong offpage SEO technique could be the big difference between where you and your competitor's feature within the SERPs.

9.1 How off-page SEO methods are able to enhance your Domain Authority (DA)

Enhancing your off-page SEO performance will directly correlate together with your Domain Authority score (DA). Note, our Site's DA is a ranking score that establishes the capability of your website to get ranking within the SERPs. This rating is from 1- 100 that is dependent upon several factors, including linking root domains, so the number of complete links. The DA of your website isn't a metric used by Google in figuring out where you rank, but it is a great sign of just how good your website is doing from an off-site SEO perspective.

Below are five off-site SEO methods you are able to follow to make sure your site has the greatest chance to enhance its domain authority, as well as ultimately rank much higher within the SERPs.

1. Creating valuable backlinks

Creating backlinks is at the center of off-site SEO and also is a method that is essential for every website together with the aspiration of ranking on the first page. Quality backlinks would be the top position factor when Google determines just where your website ranks. Google will very likely rank a website above others if one domain has extra backlinks. Moreover, Google also takes into consideration the quality of the link; a website with a greater URL that links for you is a lot more practical compared to a hyperlink from a website with a reduced DA. Nevertheless, Google's algorithm does take into account the relevancy of the hyperlink to the domain.

You will find two kinds of backlinks that may be created to enhance your off-page SEO performance:

1. Natural links: a link that is produced without any action taken. This may be either a blogger, for instance, with a good perspective towards your content and additionally links to it from their website. This particular link type could be an excellent sign of trust, endorsement, and appreciation.
2. Links created through self-promotion: These links could be made through promoting or advertising your business online. This particular link type may be accomplished by asking customers to relate to your website or even an influencer sharing your articles.

The Creation of relevant and authoritative backlinks in line together with the assistance offered by the major search engine as Google needs to be at the cutting edge of any electronic strategy. Links are going to bring referral traffic to your website, as well as Google will open your website as a trustworthy, reliable source of information. Yet link building is work that is hard and also demands a long-term strategic approach, but if done properly, the typical ranking position of your site in search results is apt to improve considerably.

2. Social Media Marketing

One of the best of off-page SEO techniques is by using social media. Making use of social media platforms is a good way to extend the access to your site content. Not merely could social media encourage far more clicks to your newest piece of content, though it is usually an important source of useful inbound links from a website with a high DA:

- LinkedIn (DA:98)
- Facebook (DA:96)
- Twitter (DA:94)
- Instagram (DA:93)

Google has not directly stated that a hyperlink from a social networking platform will profit your SEO, though they've announced that social platforms are crawled for information within the exact same way to the other website on the web.

Whilst the SEO effect of any backlink from a cultural platform remains uncertain, one certainty is your public profile's rank in the SERPs. Not merely will your social profile's ranking, they are more likely to get ranking towards the pinnacle for just about any brand-related search term. With this in mind, making sure your social profiles positively reflect your organization and what it really stands for may affect a user's very first impressions, especially in case they are not familiar together with your brand name. Moreover, amplifying insightful information through social platforms is apt to get shared, raising the likelihood and also the visibility of your material being linked to.

3. Guest Content

Provide third-party sites with guest information is another useful online advertising technique that can yield off-site SEO benefits. This may be a thought leadership piece through to' how to' video content, one thing that is going to capture the interest of the audience. You must look to meet third-party sites whose readership is akin to your own, like niche online industry publications. By doing this, you'll be rising coverage and brand recognition amongst customers and also heighten the potential for getting referral traffic from that site. Naturally, you'll also reap some benefits from an invaluable backlink. Nurturing web-based relationships through providing insightful material could be a fundamental supply of qualified traffic and also leads.

Remember, putting content on a site with a solid DA, calls for you to supply them with information or data which is completely different and is apt to have high demand from the audience.

Remember to be strategic with the websites you target to be able to place guest content, and also ensure that you're reaching out to sites that are trustworthy and appropriate to your own target market.

4. Forum Posting

A discussion board posting website is an internet discussion panel that allows users to have significant discussions really in the form of a posted message. When performed correctly, forum posting could provide several benefits for your business:

- Exposure to fresh customers
- Better understanding of your customers
- Opportunities to reply to questions some customers or customers may have

Forum posting involves a long-term strategy to be able to create a reliable reputation amongst some other members of the message board. Identifying forums having a ready-made community that are talking about a program like which you provide. This is a fantastic way of engaging with present or customers online.

Identify forums threads on topics pertinent to your company you are able to bring value to, like expert information on a certain subject to simply help answer a user's question. Where appropriate, there might, in addition function as the chance to put in a link to your site during a community discussion. Nevertheless, always make sure that this particular activity is performed sparingly, along with a backlink to your site.

5. Local Listings

Also often known as directory listings, local SEO happens to be a regular off-page SEO technique. When done properly, distributing your company into local listings is essential for improving revenue, rankings and reputation, especially in localized search results. Localized search results include many outcomes in which the person referenced an area in their search, and those in which the outcomes served are based on the user's IP address or area. The second involves searches that frequently reference phrases like' near me' or' nearby.' Local listings are mainly free and also may be very effective.

Not merely could your company benefit from an increased level of traffic and coverage, but being mentioned in local directories provides the chance of creating a valuable backlink from an impressive DA site. Many directories are famous on the net, and you're most likely already familiar with several of them:

- Google my business (DA:100)
- Foursquare (DA:92)
- Yelp (DA:70)
- Central Index (DA:58)

Submitting a local listing might seem simple, but guaranteeing you offer the same info across each listing is essential because of this off-page SEO technique. Business informations like the company name, address, and also contact number has to be the same across all listings. This might look uncomplicated, but discrepancies as abbreviations or misspellings are able to have big impacts on your listings because it is able to create confusion for Google.

In the probability of this occurring, Google might show the incorrect info or sometimes not reveal your listing at all in the SERPs.

Nevertheless, when local listings are applied properly, they could be a incredibly potent and also may provide extra business from both national and international viewers.

9.2 The best way to begin your off-site SEO strategy?

Planning out your off-site SEO strategy isn't straightforward and requires a quality of expertise and skill, note when you do not have the appropriate resource. Get in contact to understand the ideal strategy for optimizing your Sitecore Site, or reserve a digital advertising audit, andnalso evaluate your present website's performance.

We've been helping enterprise-level businesses achieve their digital goals after 1999. As a top-tier Google and Sitecore Partner, we specialize in digital advertising and work closely with all our customers on all elements of performance plus search advertising. We would be pleased to assist and discuss your project needs.

9.3 How you can Get Backlinks (15 Quick and very Simple Strategies)

Do you really want to increase the number of backlinks for your site? Backlinks play a crucial part in enhancing your search engine rankings.

It is among the top-ranking factors for Google. Plus, in case you are able to buy top-quality inbound links to your site, you have a better chance of ranking higher.

In this post, we will need to teach you how to get links using simple and quick methods. By the end of the book, you will discover great ways for link building.

What exactly are Backlinks?

Backlinks is when another site links to your site. They're also referred to as inbound backlinks and external backlinks.

Let's say a website XYZ uses your site as an outside link in a single of its content. The hyperlink from site XYZ is going to be a link for you.

So now, you might ask, how are backlinks important?

Backlinks are very beneficial for SEO (search engine optimization). They offer a vote of confidence for your site as well as your material.

Based on OptinMonster, sites with the largest quantity of backlinks often get ranking much higher on Google.

With a lot of sites linking to your website, it sends a good signal to the search engine, indicating your material provides worth, and it is linkworthy. In return, the online search engine is going to improve your website's exposure and rankings on the search engine results.

This suggests that link building is essential for your website. But how can you get backlinks for your site?

Below are 15 quick and easy strategies on how you can get backlinks. Let us dive in straight…

1. Find Backlink Opportunities with the Top Referral Sources

You can begin by looking at the best referral sources for your site— these sites which are connecting to your content and providing you a backlink.

By learning which kind of sites link to your website as well as the content type they choose, you are able to find new possibilities and also build content that is identical to obtain a backlink.

You will find various numerous ways you are able to see your referral sources. But the simplest alternative is through MonsterInsights. It is the perfect WordPress plugin for Google Analytics & presents various reports inside your WordPress dashboard.

In order to open your main referral sources, go to Insights then Reports. The very first statement you will see will likely be of Overview. Go down and also see the Top 10 Referral sources.

2. Use Outbound Links to Form Partnerships

One more method of obtaining backlink opportunities is by taking a look at your outbound links report. In case you're connecting to an impressive power site and also sending a lot of visitors, you are able to distribute an outreach email and develop a partnership.

And with MonsterInsights, you are able to quickly open your best outbound links. Simply set up the plugin and also visit Insights » Reports » Publishers and go over to Top Outbound Links report.

The article is going to show you the external links on your site which get the most clicks. You are able to then send out an email to these sites and also develop a relationship. Tell them about your content and just how you found it helpful you used it to be a source.

And you are searching for a partnership chance and possibly focus on a content effort, like a case study. If they are aboard with the concept, you are able to obtain free backlinks along with site visitors along with a connection with an industry-leading site.

3. Use Google Search Console Reports to actually get Backlinks

Google Search Console may also assist you with the way to get backlinks for your site. The totally free application by Google provides amazing details that you are able to use to enhance your rankings.

Note, among them is the External Links report. These sites that linked back to your website in the past. You are able to proceed through the inbound links and watch what content type they liked and provided you a backlink.

Because they have linked your domain in the past, they are going to be knowledgeable about your site and also may supply an additional backlink. All you've to do is find websites and reach out with content that is related.

4. Spy on Your Competitors

Ever ask yourself exactly where your competitors get their inbound links from? What are their natural strategy and what content type do they publish? When you would like to keep updated with what is occurring within the market, then you definitely ought to know what others are doing.

You are able to ethically spy on your competition to locate options for inbound links, look at their organic keywords, top-performing information, social media tasks, and much more.

To look for inbound links, you are able to use SEO tools like SEMrush. It provides a comprehensive backlink profile of any site you enter. In order to look at the backlinks in SEMrush, visit Backlink Analytics in the left panel and next get into your competitor's domain.

Now simply click Check it. Then, select Backlinks, and you will have a listing of domains from wherever your competition gets its links from.

You are able to then make use of these sources to catch a backlink to your site also. For example, in case your competition has a link from a guest blog post, you can likewise post articles on the guest posting site.

And in case they have a link from a discussion board, you are able to, in addition, develop a profile in that community and also attempt to generate a backlink.

Various other methods you can apply to keep in front of your rivals incorporate registering for their email updates and set up Google Alerts. Thus, you are instantly notified whenever they post brand new material or are featured on a different website.

5. Find Links that are Broken to Build Backlinks

While you are checking out your competitors, you can also consider their broken links. The broken link building approach is another easy and quick method of capturing backlinks.

Broken links are usually linking that do not exist or focus on a site. Plus, they could be brought on when site removing those links (also known as 404 error), have an improper URL, or the spot site may well have closed or relocated to a different domain.

Regardless of the reason, that provides an incredible chance that you can get a backlink. All you've to accomplish is locate the broken links contact the site to change the URL, and pitch your website as being an alternative. It is that simple!

In order to get brokennlinks, you should first consider your competitors then search for even more sites into your niche. Then use tools like Ahrefs or SEMrush to uncover links broken links

In SEMrush, you are able to filter the Backlinks article of your competitor. Under the various choices listed under Backlinks, check out the package for Lost. It'll next reveal to you links that greater work.

Plus, in case you are utilizing Ahrefs, now go into the site URL in its site Explorer and click Broken under the Backlinks choices from the selection in your left. The equipment is going to show you all of the broken links of your respective competitor.

When you have a listing of links that are broken, the next thing is contacting the webmaster of these sites and also the article about the broken link.

When drafting your pitch, be modest and introduce yourself. Include the actual place of the smashed link since you wish to help them out there.

Then mention various options for the broken link, such as your site. The odds are that the webmaster is going to use your site as being an alternative; also, you will get a backlink in return.

6. Create High-Quality Content that is Link-Worthy

One of the most elementary methods of how you can get backlinks is by producing top-notch content. Your goal must be to create a bit of content that different business and bloggers professionals are able to use and link to your site.

This might be a time-intensive strategy, but in case you can get it correctly, it is well worth the effort. You will find various content types you can produce. You are able to create how-to articles, list posts, create guides, and operate quizzes.

For example, in case you have a fashion blog, you create how-to posting about precisely how to manage a fashion brand with just $100 dollars. You are able to also develop a list post approximately 50 fashion trends that will reshape society.

But how can you know what content type works?

Below you are able to create MonsterInsights, getting insights. To start, you are able to check out the top landing page report to find out what pages get the most visitors, after which produce information that is identical to generate backlinks and traffic.

Plus, in case you wish to further drill down to discover what kind of articles work the very best, then you definitely are able to put together customized sizes to find out the most widely used article type.

MonsterInsights makes the process really simple, and you can see the report inside your dashboard. Simply visit Insights » Reports & select Dimensions in the top part. Then scroll down with the Most favored Post Types report.

7. Publish Skyscraper Content

When it relates to creating content, you can also create skyscraper content getting links. These intensive guides on pre-existing subjects and are really detailed and might be as long as 10,000+ words.

The concept behind a skyscraper subject material is writing an article that covers all elements of the subject in detail, and it is much better compared to the others. Thus, you are able to entice various other websites to link your blog post and produce many backlinks.

You can begin simply by looking for a subject inside your niche on Google. Then closely glimpse at the end result because they're the web pages that received a lot of backlinks and also made it with the very first page on Google.

For instance, in case you are composing content marketing, look up the search engine results. Then go through the written content on every one of the backlinks and start creating your very own post that is 10X better.

When your skyscraper written content is ready, it is time for the most crucial factor - promotion. You will find different ways or methods ways that you can to go about advertising it.

To start, you reach out to each of the people, tools, companies, influencers, and sources you outlined in your information. Tell them you found their platform being helpful, and in case they enjoyed the post, they can proceed to discuss it with their market.

As the word gets out there about your skyscraper guide, others will begin to get your content material also you will get backlinks.

Another way of advertising your post is by locating websites that have actually backlinked to existing posts then pitching your articles as a much better option.

For this, you can actually use SEO tools like Ahrefs or SEMrush. Just type in the URL of every one of the leading ten results within the device and acquire a listing of sites that provided inbound links to the original article.

Then use the list to meet these sites and also cause your skyscraper content. Explain to them the way your post is much better and push them to provide your post a link.

You can also check out more incredible content marketing examples.

8. Use Infographics to Capture Backlinks

Along with written textual content, you make use of infographics to secure backlinks for your site.

Infographics are graphic representations of information and info using charts, images, and graphics. They assist in giving a quick introduction to the subject and break down complex ideas into simple visuals, which are not hard to learn.

Consider the situation of WPBeginner. Their infographic on facts that are interesting about WordPress has more than 700 backlinks.

By creating engaging and useful infographics, you're helping other content creators. They may use a visual development of their blogs and provide you with a backlink as the initial creator of the infographic.

To produce an infographic, you do not have to be a designer or work with an expert. You are able to utilize various free online programs to create one on your own.

9. Write Testimonials

Did you realize that by writing recommendations on various other sites, you can buy a backlink for your website?

Many businesses seek out testimonials showing as social proof. They also display them on their main page.

Thus, in case you are the typical user of something or a service, you can produce a testimonial in return for a backlink. Find companies that are applicable to your market and distribute a testimonial.

Pro Tip: Look for sites with high domain authority (DA). That is because search engines consider backlinks from high DA websites to become highquality backlinks.

10. Make use of Help a Reporter Out (HARO)

When we talk of high-quality inbound links, then getting links from journalistic blogs and also news sites are similar to winning the jackpot. That is because these sites possess an impressive domain authority, and becoming featured; there'll, in addition, improve your site's trust level.

The most effective and the best way to obtain a backlink from news outlets is through Help a Reporter Out (HARO). It is a platform that offers bloggers and journalist's sources for stories and news.

In order to use HARO, subscribe to be a resource from its main page and next pick a pricing plan (you are able to work with the initial complimentary strategy to get started).

After you have signed up, you will begin getting emails from HARO with requests from various media and information sites for a quote, tips, advice, stories, and other things.

React to the queries that are applicable to your company, and in case your answer gets picked up, you will wind up getting a backlink from the media site.

11. Start Guest Blogging

Guest posting is ususally a great method to get backlinks for your site and is a tried and tested technique. You will meet various websites that accept guest blogs and publish an article.

Many sites provide a contributor account or a write for us area where anybody is able to write a page for showcased on the website. They actually allow you to relate to your website, possibly in the author bio section or within the book on the articles.

You are able to discover guest blogging sites by just running a search on Google. Write the subject keyword you wish to focus on and also put a guest post or write for contributor or us in the end. The online search engine might filter the end result and show websites that allow guest posting.

Then, draft a pitch for your subject, together with a description of what you will handle in the post. Be sure to describe the advantages and just how they can help their readers.

Guest posting helps your laser target the proper market and then create traffic to the site. You are able to find out even more by using the ultimate guide to guest blogging.

12. Take Part in Interviews

The same as a guest blog post, you can also obtain backlinks by taking part in interviews. You can end up an interview by browsing through the internet and search for websites that routinely conduct an interview.

An excellent place, to begin with, is to ask me anything. It is a site in which you answer questions in real-time about a subject. What about the bio? You are able to point out a link to your site.

One more method of landing an interview is through HARO. Just continue a search for queries that are applicable to your market and requesting a quotation or an interview.

13. Do Guest Appearances on Podcasts

You can get a free backlink out of the podcast notes in case you are able to appear as a visitor on the podcasts. As for choosing podcasts, you do exactly the same as interviews and manage a quick search for pertinent podcasts on platforms as Spotify, Google Play, iTunes, and much more.

Then distribute an email telling them you are interested in appearing as a visitor on the podcast. And be sure to add your expertise, just how you are fit for the podcast, and also the way you are able to bring value.

As soon as you begin to appear on numerous podcasts, you will also construct a following. You can then use your newly created audience in case you choose to produce a podcast on your own personal site.

14. Get involved in various Forums

Discussion forums are a good spot to look for backlinks for your website. By participating in various discussion boards, you are able to additionally turn into an industry expert and help drive visitors to your website.

In case you are uncertain what boards to get involved in, do a quick search on Google. Use any of the variants to locate related forums for your niche:

- [your niche] + forums
- Forums + [your niche]
- [your niche] + discussion

You can in addition react to issues that are different on Quora. It is a question-and-answer platform with a broad range of subjects. Just type in a search term on Quora, which is going to present you with all of the questions associated with the subject.

Another way of getting forums is by taking a look at your competitors. As we described earlier, you are able to spy on your competition to find backlinks. Using a variety of SEO tools, you can see what forums they are using to get links, and subsequently, you can to do exactly the same.

15. List your website on Resource Pages

The final approach we've for you is finding resource web pages and list your site on the web page. Resource pages are exactly where the writer curates a large list of valuable links and energy different services and products.

You can obtain a backlink by acquiring resource web pages and reaching out to the author or the website owner to mention your website on the list.

In order to look for a source page, get into your keyword on the online search engine alongside terms like helpful resource or resources list.

After you have found resource lists, contact the webmaster, and pitch your site.

Attempt personalizing your emails and also include the links to the place you would like your website to be listed. And show the way your site or tool provides value to their source page and also allows their readers.

And that is it!

You now know different ways from securing a high-quality backlink for your site. By raising the actual number of incoming links, you are able to enhance your search engine rankings.

Printed in Great Britain
by Amazon

68215625R00037